The Tales of Tippy...

A Healing Dog.

Wendy Wood-Kjelvik

Illustrated by Sarah Beilgard

ISBN-13: 978-0-578-41701-1

Library of Congress Control Number: 2018914089

Printed in the United States of America, First Printing, 2018

Wendy's Publishing House

Wendy Kjevlik
Email: kljelvik@gmail.com

DEDICATION

I dedicate this book to my dearest departed husband,
Norman Kjelvik,
without whom I would never have encountered
the star of the book, TIPPY!

ACKNOWLEDGMENTS

I wish to acknowledge the Folsom Senior Memoir Writing Class of 2018 for their enthusiastic support, and our teacher, Linda Holderness, for the guidance in writing this book. I also want to thank Sherri McCarthy of The Write Well Group in Folsom for her dedication and expertise and for which I'm forever grateful. I want to also thank Gwen Guest for assistance with this book. I want to thank Sarah Beilguard and her husband, Jim, for their artistic contributions which made my story come alive. It goes without saying that I wish to acknowledge all my dear friends who gave me unwavering encouragement to start and complete my first book. Above and beyond, I wish to thank my Lord and Savior for never failing me whenever I needed Him as well as the Bible Study group of Hope Church, Folsom, and, in particular, Alice Churchill, who comforted me and gave me the strength to accomplish this venture. I wish to acknowledge Gerald Ward, Librarian with Sacramento Public Library and in charge of the I Street Press. Last, I am forever grateful to Dr Jodi Van Tine, veterinarian and her staff for the extraordinary expertise and compassion in caring for Tippy for more than 17 years.

Table of Contents

Introduction 1

Tippy Enters Our Life 7

In Her New Home 15

Growing Up 25

Bonding and Healing 31

Healing in Many Ways 37

I Have Been Waiting for You,
My Truest Friend 41

Epilogue 49

Wendy and Red

Introduction

I never thought I would fall in love with a dog. Why is that?

When I was a toddler in India my parents bought me a dog, an Irish Red Setter named "Red," with the intent that he would be my pet, one of my play companions, and serve as a guard dog. My father was serving in the British army and was often away from our home in the barracks. Some of his duty tours took him as far as the borders of India and Burma, which were a long way from where we were stationed. Hence, he was gone for many weeks at a time. Red was part of our life during the time India was under British rule.

As a toddler, I was bent on having lots of fun with my dog, Red. I loved him and his playful manner. We had little to say to each other except for the daily toddler squeals, and the soft bark when he had had enough of me and I was taken in for my daily afternoon naps (which I hated). But come the cool of the evening, it was time for me to have fun with my favorite companion. He would grunt, bark, wag his tail, and I would squeal and laugh and hug him ever so gently. He and I were almost the same height and I was cautioned not to hug him as if to choke him. This was demonstrated to me by my mother, mostly, since my father was gone so much.

I loved putting a small wood twig near his mouth which he would then dutifully grab and run around in circles, his tail wagging until he dropped the twig at my feet. We repeated this play often. Eventually he would lie down and put his face on the cool grass. That was the signal for me to sit next to him and be quiet. He was my best friend and I truly looked forward to our daily play time. I was not afraid of him.

Our happy routine changed one day when I handed him a twig, and he suddenly bit me on my wrist. I was very startled and frightened to the point of screaming. I sobbed and crumpled to the grass. I don't remember much else of that day.

What I do remember is being in a hospital and the pain of undergoing a series of 40 anti-rabies injections in my tiny abdomen. In India in the early 1940s, the treatment for a dog bite was injections. It was assumed all dogs could be carrying rabies. It was also custom to put a biting dog to sleep. So, my dog, Red, was immediately put to sleep. I was truly heartbroken when I was told in baby toddler language that Red had "gone to heaven." My best friend was gone, and in the midst of feeling sadness and loss, I also became afraid of all dogs. This fear of dogs lasted for over 40 years.

For over 40 years I avoided contact with dogs, and even environments where dogs would be. I avoided parks in India, London, and Chicago, cities where I worked as a nurse. I cultivated wonderful friends, many of whom had a pet dog or a cat. They knew that I was not a "dog-friendly" person and they treasured my friendship so much that when I would visit them, they kindly put their dog in another room. I felt many times if I could just get over this fear and aversion to dogs, I could be a better friend. I would buy their dogs gifts, but most of them were inappropriate. I was so lacking in the knowledge of a dog's world.

I was extremely ambitious in my professional life, and I had no thoughts about dogs. However, there were instances in those 40 years when I was mildly curious, but still afraid.

A very dear friend of mine in Chicago, Trudy, had a Doberman named Joe. Trudy and I met while playing tennis. I admired her talents and my husband at the time, Bill, and I became lifelong friends with her and her husband, Max. Bill loved children and dogs, and when we visited Max and Trudy, Joe would zoom right to him, licking him voraciously. Meantime, I was petrified. I would quietly and quickly remove myself to another room. I struggled with my fears of him, carefully avoiding him every time we visited. Trudy understood, and I was grateful for her understanding.

Then, after 40 years of fear, a dog named Tippy came into my life. Her capacity to heal me of my fears and bring me joy was like a small miracle. It was a major "Life Changer." This is the story of her life and a testament to her capacity to heal the people she loved and adored.

Chapter 1:

Tippy Enters Our Life

One Sunday morning my husband, Norm, received a phone call from his daughter inviting him to come see her new puppies. Norm agreed and informed me that *we* were going to see puppies. I protested. When I said I was not interested in looking at puppies, Norm suggested I accompany him for the drive, as she lived in the country. I agreed to the drive through the country, but my heart was not warmed by the thought of looking at puppies. You see, I was still afraid of dogs, even puppies. Once we arrived and he strode off to see the puppies, I am not sure why I hesitatingly followed.

The smallest puppy waddled over to Norman's shoe like a curious duckling, nestled into the laces and looked up at him with deep black eyes. He stood very still, fearing if he moved she would fall and hurt herself on the cold concrete garage floor where the puppy lived with her mother and a sibling. She was very busy being cute, chewing the laces and licking his shoe. She had a black coat that had the appearance of mink and a blaze of white fur in the shape of a triangle on her chest. Her paws looked as though they had been dipped in white paint, and she had a white tip on her tail, which wagged nonstop. Norman was entranced by her and I watched an immediate friendship blossom between them.

At first, I looked at her thinking how harmless and adorable she seemed. Then, I remembered my sad experience with my childhood dog, Red, but quickly put it out of my mind. I saw the delight in Norm's eyes as he watched her, and I quietly said to him, "Don't you think the puppy just *has* to be named Tippy?" "Yes," he replied in firm agreement.

Tippy was one of two lucky puppies who survived from a litter of nine. We were told all nine puppies were alive at birth but only she and her sister survived and were now nine weeks old. Tippy surely had an angel watching over her. Norm's daughter was anxious to have Tippy adopted, which I feared was about to happen. Sure enough, Norman picked Tippy up, cuddled her, and announced she was going home with us. While *he* was certain, I was still hesitant about this decision and reminded Norm I had lived with a fear of dogs all my life.

You see, when I was a toddler living with my parents in India, my very own pet dog, Red, bit me by accident. The bite was treated by forty anti-rabies injections into my stomach, and the pain lived in my memory ever since. I also felt a sense of loss when Red was put to sleep. I thought about him often over the years. Instead of fond thoughts of my friend, my thoughts became the seeds of a fear of all dogs. This fear was something I handled as best I could, but I knew Norm wanted a dog. It seemed so clear that he truly wanted Tippy as part of our family, and so, quite reluctantly, I agreed.

Norm placed Tippy in a shoebox and gently put the shoebox on my lap for the journey home. She cried all the way, only falling asleep when we arrived at our house. Norm declared Tippy would be a fine "outside" dog because he had owned similar "outside" dogs in his early years on a farm in Northern Minnesota. I asked what "outside" meant. He explained that the puppy would live for the time being in our garage, which was attached to the house, and eventually she would live "outside" in the yard.

I looked down at Tippy, sound asleep in the shoe box, and noted how tiny she was. "Could she really ever live outside all by herself?" I thought. I protested to Norm that perhaps the garage was too cold a place for such a tiny creature. After all, she had just been removed from the warmth and safety of her mother and was still just a puppy.

Norm did not see things the same way, as his life on the farm had always included dogs that lived "outside."

It was getting late and both of us had to get up early the next morning so Tippy was placed in her box in the garage, and off to bed we went. In less than an hour, I heard Tippy crying, and my heart pounded, wondering what to do. The crying became more desperate. I just had to do something. I looked over at Norm, who was fast asleep and snoring. I crept out of bed and headed toward the garage.

First, I sat inside by the garage door near the kitchen, and immediately the crying stopped. I thought perhaps Tippy was missing the warmth of her mother, so I decided to sit by the door for the rest of the night to calm her and make her feel better. Norm had said earlier that "outside" dogs learn quickly to adapt to being on their own "outside." I was torn between my childhood feelings of fear and a sudden feeling of warm love washing over my mind. I fell into a shallow sleep. Tippy startled me awake by crying mournfully, as if her heart was breaking. This sound had an instant effect on me and I, who knew very little about puppies, became bold and decisive. I decided to abandon Norm's "outside" dog theories. I opened the door and brought Tippy in her box into the kitchen.

Tippy scrambled to one side of the box, stretched up, and began clawing at the top edges, forcing the box to topple, and landing in a soft heap right on my lap!

I trembled, unsure what to do at this moment. She whimpered and stared at me sadly. I realized she, too, was frightened, and was begging for attention and love. Overcoming my fears, I picked her up and wrapped her gently in a dry kitchen towel. Tippy immediately began to lick my hands and every part of my face her soft, pink tongue could reach. I gently touched her head and neck as she moaned, looking at me with complete trust and love. My eyes and heart absorbed everything about her innocent face, knowing she had nobody but Norm and me in her big "new world." All the while, she thoroughly studied *me* with her deep, dark, loving, and healing eyes seemingly saying, "Don't be afraid of me."

Chapter 2:

In Her New Home

As dawn lit up the sky, Tippy and I had survived our first night in her new home. My fear of dogs amazingly began to fade. I looked at her and saw her little black eyes staring at me expectantly as if to say "Mummy, I'm so hungry. Please, can I have something to eat soon?" I quickly realized we had no puppy food in the house, and I began to panic. My mind raced, and I tried to determine what I could give her to eat. It would have to be human food, but what food would be least harmful to a puppy?

Adrenaline pumping in my body, I reached for an egg in the refrigerator. I thought perhaps if I scrambled it, surely it would be acceptable. Out of the corner of my eye I saw Tippy take a few steps toward me and sit on her haunches, her head tipped to one side, her eyes watching my every move. This was one of her ways to communicate that she expected me to rise to the occasion, and her eyes showed complete trust that no harm would come of my actions.

I quickly scrambled the egg, blew it to a cool temperature, and served it to her on a china plate. Yikes! We did not even have dog dishes! She ate the egg as quick as a breath, wagging her tail joyfully. A bit of egg stuck on her nose. I gently wiped it away. She licked my hand in spurts with her warm, little tongue, and when finished she again sat back on her haunches and looked expectantly for? For what I was not certain. I supposed now she needed a drink of water. I got another china bowl, filled it up, and placed it down before her. She dived into the bowl, making so much noise slurping up the water, I thought she would surely wake Norm. Then, before I could blink an eye, she darted across the kitchen floor, slipping as she ran, her white-tipped tail wagging. She made quick headway down the white carpeted corridor, heading directly for Norm, who was still sleeping soundly.

I quickly pursued her and reached her in time to see her sit at the side of the bed and look up at his sleeping form. I was about to scoop her up in to my arms when she decided it was time to relieve her bladder right into one of his bedroom slippers! Horrified, I picked her up in the wet slipper and began retreating to the kitchen as quickly as I could. I made it to the hallway when Norm suddenly awoke, swung his legs on to the floor, feeling for his slippers. I glanced at him from the hallway with Tippy peeking curiously at me from the warm wet slipper in my hand. I heard him mutter, "where is my one slipper?" Instantly, my mind flashed to the movie "My Fair Lady" in which Professor Higgins was searching for his slippers and cried out "Eliza, where the Dickens are my slippers?" I thought this was it for Tippy and me! What explanation could I give him that would be appropriate after I disregarded his "outside" dog theory and brought Tippy inside the house? I swallowed hard and continued my journey to the garage.

Sensing we were both in trouble, I quickly separated Tippy from the slipper and threw it in the dryer. I wrapped Tippy in a laundry towel, whispered "STAY" in her ear, and placed her on the garage floor. She blinked at me, whimpering as if to say, "I'm sorry." The door to the garage opened and there stood Norm. He seemed larger than life from where I was crouching on the floor with Tippy. I can imagine he looked like a giant to Tippy.

I nonchalantly enquired as to whether he had a good night's sleep. Peering over his glasses, he nodded, walked over to pet Tippy, and returned the question as to whether we had a good night's sleep. I must have looked less than well rested, but Tippy stood up, head to one side, wagging her tail furiously as if to say, "It was one tough night for both of us, Master, but my Mistress is not going to let that happen again." Gaining courage from her unspoken words, I announced in a firm voice, "Tippy will from now and forever be an 'INSIDE' DOG!"

He followed me into the house with a grin on his face and murmured, "Well then, we have our work cut out for us now that we are parents of Tippy." I did not fully comprehend what work training a dog entailed as I proceeded to get ready for my job at the hospital. Whilst doing so, I turned to find Tippy watching intently as I put on my clothes. She sat on her haunches, her head cocked to one side, and let out an enormous yawn. I, too, was tired and a bit jumpy, having had a unique and sleepless night. I was not used to piercing black eyes watching my every move as I got dressed.

Norm called for Tippy, and she took off like a black streak down the white carpeted corridor. I followed her and saw Norm open the kitchen door leading to the garage. Tippy followed obediently. I thought he was going to let her play out in the garden while we went to work. Not so. He watched her while she relieved herself on a patch of grass and then took off sniffing her way to every tree, wagging her tail. Eventually she scampered back and parked herself right by his shoes. I watched the sequence of events and realized we had spent almost 15 minutes getting this ritual completed. It then occurred to me that this is what we would have to do at least five or six times a day and even, perhaps, at night. Training a dog was going to take a lot of time.

Norm silently petted Tippy, whose tail never stopped wagging. He said good bye and took off for work. Tippy looked at me, head cocked to one side. I wondered what she would say if she could speak. I gingerly petted her head and wondered what to do. The thought struck me that I could not leave her here at the house by herself. An impulse suddenly overcame me, and I darted to the phone to call my manager at the hospital. I requested a few days off for "Dog Maternity Leave." At first, she giggled and enquired as to whether I was OK. I could visualize her perplexed expression since she and I had discussed many times my not liking and fearing dogs. And here I was, requesting maternity leave as though I had given birth to one! Permission for a few days off was granted, and I was greatly relieved.

Tippy seemed to know all was well. She scampered around the house, and then placed herself at my feet as I formulated a plan on how I was going to become a co-parent of a dog. She licked my shoe and wagged her tail. I looked at her shyly now that we were alone, and my thoughts drifted back to Red. Tippy was so little now, but I knew she would grow bigger. I wondered if I would grow to love her like I loved Red, and whether it would ever happen that she would suddenly bite me out of the blue. I suddenly felt anxious, and Tippy immediately sat up, cocked her head to one side, and looked into my eyes. It felt as though her black eyes were looking into my soul and saying "Don't be afraid of me. I'm here for you."

The phone rang and brought me abruptly back to reality. It was Norm enquiring if I was going to work that day. He was assured I decided to stay home with Tippy. He said he would come home for lunch to relieve me of my dog-parent duties and reminded me to take Tippy out to the garden and tell her to go "pee pee." I hung up and took her out, but she would not do anything but sit right by my feet. I came into the house with her following right behind me. She found china dishes we had used earlier and started licking them. It was time to feed her again. This time, instead of eggs, I covered my car's passenger seat with a towel to prevent another slipper incident, and together we took off to the grocery store for dog provisions. She sat quietly watching every move I made and eventually fell asleep on her towel.

Tippy slept blissfully in the car with the windows slightly ajar while I proceeded into the pet shop, finally buying the most expensive puppy food. My instinct led me to buy the best for her since she was my "puppy child." REALLY! I was transforming into a DOG parent.

She awoke as I opened the door to the car with the food and supplies. She sat up and her piercing black eyes sparkled. Her tail wagged as she leaped in to my lap and licked my face in unabashed joy. "Hmm," I thought as I reined in my feeling of ultimate pleasure that someone was so appreciative of me.

I replaced my good China dishes with new, dog-appropriate stainless-steel bowls. I smiled as I gave her a cup full of her new food and filled her water bowl with fresh water. Tippy's tail never stopped wagging as she dived in to her gourmet meal. I stood by watching in awe. It was a simple deed for which I received unconditional love. I started to breathe deep with a simple smile. The warmth I experienced was so new.

Norm came home at lunch and explained he had taken the rest of the day off from work to help with Tippy. This was a great relief as we needed to have a serious talk about how we would manage Tippy and our jobs. Tippy placed herself in between our respective feet with her ears perked up, listening to our conversation. I never would have thought I would feel this way about being a serious parent after so many years of fearing dogs. I was confident, though, that Norm would be the lead, Alpha parent since he had experience raising a dog.

Tippy lay between our feet and napped. It was a nice feeling to have a dog just lie there contently and show she loved us both with her easy breath. Norm quickly planned a schedule for us to follow. For the next 4 months we would leave her for 1-3 hours during our work days and take turns returning home to walk her and play with her. Norm built a dog door to allow her to go out to the garden to relieve herself whilst we were home, and whilst we were gone. He emphasized to me that we had to be consistent with commands such as "come," "stay," "sit," "good dog," "no," and we should very rarely use the words "bad dog."

Our schedule worked well. I was so proud of her for not having any accidents in the house, especially since our white carpet was new. She also never dug outside in the garden and did not get up on the furniture or chew on anything but her toys. She waited by the kitchen door for our return every day.

Norm naturally took on the role of the Alpha parent, and I easily assumed the role of being the play companion and supported his dog rearing techniques. After a few months, Tippy was an obedient, loving, and entertaining puppy. Who would have thought I, who once feared dogs so badly, would fall in love with a dog called Tippy? Already, in her first months of life, she had begun my healing journey through her gentle ways, loving behavior, and intent black eyes that massaged my soul, which needed healing desperately.

Chapter 3:

Growing Up

Tippy grew quickly from a minute, black, furry, ball into a vibrant, active puppy with an ever-wagging tail. The days were exhausting for both Norm and me but compared to some horror stories told by friends whose puppy days were a nightmare, our dog was amazingly quick to obey all commands.

One day, we were both very tired and retired to bed, forgetting we had left the garage door to the backyard open. Tippy usually slept in her bed on the floor at the end of our bed. That night, for some reason, I suddenly awoke and realized she was gone. Searching the house with no success, I quickly went out to the backyard, which was pitch dark. I switched on the outside light and there was Tippy, standing perfectly still in the vegetable bed, her tail pointed straight, the fur on her back standing up, growling in a menacing manner. For one split second, my fear of dogs returned. I panicked until my eyes landed on what looked like a huge feral cat, who was twice the size of Tippy, ready to pounce at her. My own fear was gone, replaced with the urgency to protect my Tippy. I screamed and ran toward them but slipped and fell on the wet lawn. Tippy started to bark at the cat in a deep voice, one that I had never heard. The cat cowered and soon disappeared into the darkness. Tippy bounded over and landed on top of my head. Her body was shaking, but she was determined to lick every part of my face in between little whimpers. In the muted light, her eyes were intent on mine, as if to say, "Thanks Mom. I was only protecting you and Dad from the monster."

I, like her, was shaking with the thought that Tippy might have been killed by the huge wild cat. She sat on her haunches looking at me and I knew then that my fears were never coming back. She had proven she was my protector and she loved me. The bond between us grew even stronger. She was healing me of past fears and memories. Her love gave me hope. She wagged her tail and followed me back inside, as if it was all in a day's work.

That incident taught Norm and me a lesson about being more vigilant to check doors at night. Our backyard was open to an orchard with no protective fence, so all kinds of animals were tempted to prowl about at night. We decided perhaps it was time to look for a more dog-friendly house with a secure backyard.

Three months later, we fell upon the house of our dreams in Folsom. Tippy was one year old. We celebrated both the new house and Tippy's birthday. Tippy was particularly happy because in addition to a fenced backyard, we also had access to a nice park at the end of the street. That meant Tippy could be walked as many times as needed, and she was safe.

When winter came, we bought a bright yellow hooded, full body rain coat for Tippy. It was difficult to put it on her as her body wiggled with excitement when she saw the coat. She knew it was time to go for a walk, even if it was raining, and her tail wagged with joy. It was almost like I was a mother trying to dress my child. I was reminded again how her personality and her unconditional love had healed me and allowed me to experience a range of emotions I had never known. We also bought her a red ball that lit up once she put it into her mouth. She dutifully carried the ball in her mouth every time we took her for a walk.

Her routine began when she reached her favorite tree. She would take a big sniff, turn around and drop the ball at my feet. Then, she would take a step back, lower her body to a crouching position and wait for me to pick it up and throw it as far as I could. She would run as fast as a hare, leaping into the air, and grabbing the ball. We did this several times on every walk, come rain or shine. When she tired herself out, she would drop to the grass, panting furiously. That was the signal to go home. Once we were in the house, she would dart to her water bowl and slurp noisily, tail wagging, as if to say, "Thank you so much!" Little did Tippy know that this routine of walking several times a day helped Norm and me to stay fit and healthy.

Chapter 4:

Bonding and Healing

Over the next few years Tippy lived as our best friend and my fear of dogs was almost forgotten. I say almost because I had to learn lessons about "other" dogs when they visited us and when we were out on walks. We chose to keep Tippy leashed when we walked, only allowing her off leash on a small area in the park near our house so she could chase the little red ball. We kept a close watch for approaching dogs, and if we saw one, we immediately put her back on leash.

One balmy, summer morning during our routine walk, she was trotting along, tail wagging, ball in mouth. Out of nowhere a pit bull charged toward us, no owner in sight. I was very startled and afraid. As the dog lunged to attack Tippy's neck, I shot out my left hand to protect Tippy, only to have the dog's teeth dig in to my wrist in a vicious grip. I fell over Tippy with the other dog hanging onto my wrist. I let out a gut-wrenching scream which momentarily startled the dog and allowed me to snatch my wrist out of its mouth. I was still holding onto Tippy and the leash when the owner of the dog appeared, nonchalantly talking on her cell phone. After leashing her dog, she explained that "he is just a puppy and wanted to play with your dog." I responded in a shaken voice, "A badly behaved one, all the same!"

Tippy was shaking like a leaf but kept licking my left wrist, which I had no idea was bleeding. We went home, and I cleaned up the wound. Tippy, panting with nerves, watched every move. She groaned as I stroked her ears, looked her straight in the eye and said, "I will always protect you, my dear friend. After all, I'm your mummy."

When she chose to lie at my feet that evening rather than her usual spot near Norm, he was confused. Tippy put her head between her paws as I explained the incident to him. It was as if she were trying to say it was her fault I got bit. That night, she slept on the cold tile floor near my side of the bed instead of in her warm doggie bed.

We had formed an even deeper bond as a result of the unfortunate incident, and future days walking her included even more watchfulness, being very wary of "other dogs."

Tippy was a well-loved, neighborhood dog, often referred to as "Queen" Tippy. She was very patient with children, who loved to stroke her beautiful mink-like coat. She did not let any dog come near Norm and me, and if she was on leash, we kept her away from other dogs as well. She became a "people" dog and I often wondered if she missed what dogs were supposed to do to communicate with each other, but it was only a momentary thought.

She acted like a person in other ways, too. On occasion, Norm and I would listen to music and he would play guitar and sing along with some country and western songs. I remember a time he got up and came to me, bowed slightly and asked me to dance. He was an excellent dancer and I was very awkward. Tippy stood right by us, tail wagging as if she approved. Well, it always happened when we danced that he would mutter softly "I'm the lead and you must follow." My awkward dancing abilities would eventually lead him to sigh, and the dance would stop.

But, on one occasion, after my dance with Norm ended, I walked over to Tippy, who had been watching with her tail wagging furiously. I bowed to her and asked her if she would like to dance. I gently held up her front paws and we trotted around the floor for a few seconds dancing like a circus act. Norm said with a wry smile, "You are so silly!" We may have been silly, but we made great dance partners because we had similar dancing abilities. After our dance, Tippy rested her head between Norm and me, tail wagging, and we both stroked her head and ran our fingers down her back. She loved our touch and we loved to shower her with our love. That was just one of many great, playful evenings, and I remember them now with such joy.

Tippy also loved guests. When someone new came to our home, she would tear around the living room floor grabbing a toy and gently dropping it at the foot of the unsuspecting guest. She would engage the guest in the "throw and fetch game." It was her way of saying to Linda, Duke, Margery, Jackie, Carol, Kathy, Harry, Kim, Mike, Kyle and so many others, "I'm so happy you are here, and I love you!"

Tippy had a particular fondness for our friend, Jackie. When Jackie stayed overnight, Tippy, our "dog ambassador," would sneak into her bedroom and stare at her until Jackie moved. Then, playing resumed until Tippy was completely satisfied that Jackie was alive and well.

Tippy accompanied Norm and me on several road trips as far as Canada. I will never forget how she would not drink much water when she knew we off on a trip. She would settle in the back seat behaving well, but Norm would often want to stop for a potty break, and Tippy would let out this long groan as if to comment, "Really? Do we have to stop again?" In other words, "I want to get to where we are going, guys!" Once we made it to our destination, she was quiet as a mouse and adjusted to sleeping in strange places without any problems. She was a great travel dog and we were so happy to take her places so long as she got her walks, her food and her treats and timely potty stops.

Tippy began to slow down as she approached her thirteenth birthday. As a Labrador/Border Collie mix, her dog-age was in cadence with Norm's age. As his hair turned gray, so did both her muzzle and her eyebrows. Her onyx eyes never lost their sparkle and she continued to do her usual panting as if to say, "Let's go for a walk, please guys." Her teeth stayed as white as snow by a weekly teeth cleaning with chicken-flavored toothpaste.

Norm eventually became frail in health. Tippy sensed he needed her undivided attention when they were at home together. Their close relationship would pay dividends in the future.

Chapter 5:

Healing in Many Ways

Tippy, although getting on in years, never gave up on her requests for walks. She would stand by the door, vigorously wagging her tail. This routine happened at least twice a day. Nowadays on our walks, she would sniff out any other dog's pee on various bushes, lampposts, and trees. She would then make her own mark with a healthy squirt. Each time this occurred, she trotted off with a sigh of accomplishment, looking at us for approval. After all, this is behavior we learned is part of a dog's purpose in life.

She became more attentive to Norm. We would soon witness her transform into his on-site health protector. One day, he was reading his morning paper, which was his regular routine. She always sat on her bed, her head between her front legs, watching and waiting for the moment the paper would be put down. She knew once the paper was down, he would rise and head into the kitchen where he would put his cereal in a bowl, and cover it lavishly with rich cream. She followed him expectantly as she knew there would be some delicious cream left for her when he was through.

Today, however, something different happened. Whilst reading his paper, Norm's hands dropped suddenly, the newspaper fell to the floor, and his head rolled back on the couch. Tippy immediately leapt off her bed, pounced on his thighs, barked furiously at him, and panted into his mouth. She sensed something was wrong with her master. Although the incident lasted less than a minute, her quick action brought him back from what was later diagnosed as a transient ischemic accident (TIA), a small stroke.

Norm survived on account of Tippy's innate ability to sense a medical crisis. Norm was a very lucky man, and his doctor was able to treat him with medications to prevent future episodes. Our veterinarian explained to us that Tippy was essentially a medical alert dog. She had skills inherent in some dogs, which are a valuable gift. She was given a badge to wear on her collar. She wore it humbly, somehow knowing she carried more responsibility than just an ordinary pet dog. It was as if both master and pet were always meant to be on a lifelong trajectory together. Norm was so lucky to have Tippy as his medical alert dog.

Chapter 6:

I Have Been Waiting for You, My Truest Friend

Swish, swish, glug, glug are the noises Tippy made when drinking water. She followed the noisy drinking with a healthy shake of her head, water droplets flying in all directions, covering the floor and anything within range of her head. Our home had tile floors, so we had to be sure to mop the area around her food and water bowl, drying the pathway of droplets, lest we slip and fall.

She started to drink water more frequently as she entered her 14th birthday. She drank so much that we filled her bowl at least four times a day. We had to make sure her water bowl was full before we went to bed because she would drink all through the night. Even today, I still sometimes wake up from my sleep and think I hear her drinking even though she has not been here in over three years! I mentioned her new water habit to her veterinarian as well as the fact that she was using the dog door three times more often. I suspected she might have diabetes but that was not the case. What she had was Cushing's syndrome due to a tumor on her adrenal glands. The news was startling.

Despite her disease, Tippy was a happy and ever-loving dog. She continued her happy ways even with high levels of cortisol racing around in her blood stream, causing high blood pressure and feelings of panic. When she started to pant excessively, Norm and I decided to seek more treatment for her disease. Tippy's veterinarian was qualified in both western and eastern medicine, which is unusual. Treatment was our choice: either surgery to remove the tumor or feeding her Chinese herbs and monitoring her cortisol levels through blood tests every three months. We chose the Chinese herb form of treatment. It took several days before the levels of cortisol started to drop, and two months before it was anything near normal.

The challenge for us during this time was how to disguise the herbs so she would ingest them with her meals. We tried every trick, but she somehow always knew her food was contaminated with the herbs. She would stare at her food, sigh, groan, and walk away. Her vet suggested disguising the herbs in rolled up pieces of deli turkey lined with a smear of peanut butter as a treat rather than putting them in her food. She would quickly take one slice of plain deli turkey meat, which allowed us to then give her the second slice, armed with the Chinese herbs. Since we had never routinely given her treats, she would put her head to one side and look at us with a question as if to ask, "Why, all of a sudden, are you being so nice to me with all these treats twice a day, every day?"

We developed a routine to prepare the Chinese herb treats. We would roll the meat in paper towels and take it to the garage to insert the peanut butter and herbs. Once we came in, we would ignore her for about ten minutes to keep her from being suspicious. After that time passed, one of us would go into the refrigerator, take the deli turkey, command her to "SIT." When she had done what we asked, we gave her the "treat." This routine was the only way Tippy would willingly take her medications for the disease.

Tippy was a smart dog and if Norm forgot this routine whilst I was at work, Tippy did not get her medication, which altered her blood cortisol levels. As Norm began to age, he started having more forgetful moments. Tippy would follow him wherever he went, including the bathroom. It was on one of these occasions that she again saved his life. I was in the office in the back of the house when she came tearing in, barking furiously. I immediately checked her water bowl, which was full. She continued to jump up and down without wagging her tail, but I could not figure out why she was so upset. Desperately, she grabbed my pant leg and started pulling me in the direction of the bathroom where I found Norm sprawled on the floor, semi-conscious!

I shook him and, with the other hand, called 911. Tippy continued barking at Norm between her licks to his bleeding forehead. Norm groaned and looked up at me. Tippy went to the front door to welcome the fire department medics with a resounding bark and wagging tail. If that tail of hers could tell a tale, one would be amazed.

Norm had the first of many MRIs of the brain that day. He was informed by his doctor to keep Tippy with him wherever he went. Even the bathroom.

Tippy, now 17, had turned completely gray on her muzzle and eyebrows. She was an old dog by all accounts. Even so, when Norm had a serious fall, Tippy was right there beside him, ministering to him. Norm made another trip to the hospital. Tippy waited by the window with an expectant look, hoping for him come home to her. Meantime, at the hospital, Norm was off the ventilator, breathing on his own, and looking very peaceful.

I had been with Norm, his family, and good, loyal friends Linda, Diane, Judy, Char and Kathy at the hospital for close to 18 hours. Norm had suffered a massive brain bleed and we knew it would be fatal. I was exhausted and very anxious about Tippy being alone at the house. I needn't have worried because neighbors looked in on her, fed her, and walked her. I finally left the hospital for a short break to get some rest. I returned home to Tippy. I sat in the dark house, and I was so tired I drifted off to sleep with Tippy's head in my lap. I was awakened around 4 am by Tippy's horrific groan just as the phone rang with the news that Norm had passed away. I took her head in my hands whilst I cried. She licked all the tears from my face and let out small whimpers, as if she knew that Norm (Papa to her) was gone forever.

I became her only parent. Her sadness at our loss weighed heavily on her. Six months later, she was diagnosed with a very fast-growing blood cancer. You would never know how sick she was by her behavior. Otherwise normal, she started to avoid her food and lost weight rapidly. She was medicated for pain to keep her comfortable. One day, on our usual walk, she stopped and looked at me, turned and walked slowly to our house. She looked so sad and so tired, I called her veterinarian who asked me to bring her in immediately, which I did. I never expected this would result in Tippy being "put down" within the hour. All the staff surrounded her, each one gently massaging her and whispering in her ears. Her veterinarian of 17 years and 6 months lovingly administered the fatal injection to end her pain.

Through her final seconds, she never stopped looking at me. Upon her death, I immediately had a vision of her frolicking up a golden ladder into the sky. At the top of the ladder stood Norm, gathering her into his arms, kissing the tip of her head, whilst saying, "I have been waiting for you my truest friend."

Epilogue

I fell in love with a dog called Tippy. I never would have believed I would transform from a person who feared dogs into a dog lover. It could not have happened if it weren't for Tippy. She was an extraordinary creature and she was so much a part of my life that today, four years after she passed, I still ache for her presence.

She healed me, and it was quite clear during her life that she was a health protector for Norm. She earned the badge as a medical alert dog and she never let Norm down. She never let me down, either.

She taught me the power of love and her very special, unique gift healed me of fear.

I hope one day to see her again but until then, I know she and Norm are happy together. The feelings I carry that come with having a dog's unconditional love sustain me.

My hope is for all who read this book to seek a course leading to the unbelievably rich and rewarding experience I had with Tippy. I encourage readers to support local pet shelters. All net proceeds from the sale of this book will benefit the Sacramento SPCA.

Last, I would ask, "Would you like to fall in love with a dog?"

ABOUT THE AUTHOR

 Wendy currently lives in Northern California. She is a semi-retired registered nurse, and a Patron of charities associated with animals, children and dance. She currently volunteers with the Good News Club, an after-school program at a local elementary school.

This is her first book although she has successfully published many nursing articles. She has a large network of loyal friends across the USA and the UK. She keeps in close touch with her brother, Richard, and his family living in Australia. She is involved with members of Norman's family in California, Wisconsin, North Dakota and Minnesota.

Wendy's dog, Tippy, has been her only pet in the USA and is resting peacefully under a bountiful lemon tree in her friend Linda's back yard in Fair Oaks, CA. She can be reached at kljelvik@gmail.com